WEST CORNWALL SMUGGLERS' PUBS

St Ives to Falmouth

Terry Townsend

To my wife Carol
for in every sense this is her book, too

ACKNOWLEDGEMENTS

Thanks also to Adrienne Bradney-Smith
and Brenda and Tony Stables
for their continued help and support

Terry Townsend's other Halsgrove titles include:
Once upon a Pint – A Readers' Guide to the Literary Pubs & Inns of Dorset & Somerset,
Kent Smugglers' Pubs, Dorset Smugglers' Pubs, Jane Austen's Hampshire,
Jane Austen & Bath, Jane Austen's Kent, Hampshire Smugglers' Pubs, Isle of Wight
Smugglers' Pubs, Bristol & Clifton Slave Trade Trails

First published in Great Britain in 2017

Copyright © Terry Townsend 2017

All rights reserved. No part of this publication
may be reproduced, stored in a retrieval system,
or transmitted in any form or by any means
without the prior permission of the copyright
holder.

British Library Cataloguing-in-Publication Data
A CIP record for this title is available from the
British Library

ISBN 978 0 85710 108 2

PiXZ Books
Halsgrove House, Ryelands Business Park,
Bagley Road, Wellington, Somerset TA21 9PZ
Tel: 01823 653777
Fax: 01823 216796
email: sales@halsgrove.com

An imprint of Halstar Ltd, part of the
Halsgrove group of companies
Information on all Halsgrove titles is
available at: www.halsgrove.com

Printed and bound in India by
Parksons Graphics

CONTENTS

ST IVES
BAY

CAMBORNE

ST IVES ①

Cornwall

PENRYN

FALMOUTH

② ⑰

ST JUST

⑧ PENZANCE

⑨ HELSTON

⑦ ⑪

③ ⑥ ⑩ ⑯

④ ⑤ ⑮

AND'S
END

MOUNT'S BAY

⑫

⑬

⑭

LIZARD POINT

Even on a bright sunny day the old inn retains a foreboding presence.

Prologue

On a cold, eerie night in 1930, twenty-three-year-old Daphne du Maurier arrived with a girl friend at Jamaica Inn, high on windswept Bodmin Moor. The following day the two young women went riding but, on their return as the light was fading, mist suddenly descended leaving them disorientated. Lost and frightened they had the inspiration to dismount hoping their horses would lead them back; thankfully they did.

Staying on a few more nights to recover from the ordeal Daphne learned about the inn's celebrated history and involvement in smuggling. Deeply impressed by the ancient hostelry and wild deserted moor she was inspired to write her famously compelling novel, *Jamaica Inn*.

I was about Daphne's age when I read the story of orphan Mary Yellan going to live with her Aunt Patience and sinister

Uncle Joss Merlyn, the inn's landlord. I was absorbed with the mystery surrounding Merlyn's involvement in smuggling and wrecking along the Cornish coast and like hundreds of readers before and since, couldn't wait to visit the inn for myself.

On this first, and subsequent visits, I have not been disappointed despite the fact things have inevitably changed. There is now a coach park, Smugglers' Museum and gift shop as large as the bar, but somehow the authentic old place retains a sense of foreboding and a timeless presence in a changing world. The atmosphere that captured Du Maurier's imagination, conveyed by the harsh granite exterior, cobbled courtyard, and dimly-lit low-beamed interior, is still accessible for those who are receptive to its mood.

It seems the sign writer had *Treasure Island* in mind, rather than Daphne du Maurier's classic tale of Cornish smugglers and wreckers.

For me the experience sparked a lifelong interest in smuggling and smugglers' pubs from Kent to Cornwall and a desire to share my discoveries in a series of books. This is the first in a two-volume exploration of Cornish Smugglers' Pubs. I hope you enjoy reading it as much as I have enjoyed researching and writing it.

Terry Townsend

Throughout the smuggling era Cornwall was a land set apart from the rest of England with its own language, traditions and culture.

Introduction

A World Apart

Throughout the smuggling era Cornwall was a land set apart from the rest of England. Virtually surrounded by sea and severed from the mainland by the River Tamar, it is almost an island. Two hundred years ago it thought of itself as another country with its own language, traditions and culture. From Cornwall it was a five-day stagecoach journey to London. The Cornish people regarded the rest of the population with suspicion and the feeling was mutual.

Cornish men and women had little regard for central government or for a remote King who imposed huge taxes on imported luxuries to meet the cost of his foreign wars. The practice of taxation on exports and imports began as early as the thirteenth century. By the eighteenth century duties were levied on a vast range of imported goods including tea, brandy, silks, muslins, handkerchiefs and 'salt', essential for the Cornish fishing industry.

Liquid Gold

Cornwall's southern fishing communities had depended on catching one particular type of fish – pilchards; also known as sardines, or locally as liquid gold! The fortunes of the fisher folk depended on a tiny window of opportunity between the late summer and early autumn when shoals of the little fish appeared around the south coast.

Cornwall's southern fishing communities depended on catching pilchards, known locally as liquid gold!

The vast majority of Cornish pilchards were exported to the Mediterranean, requiring tons of salt for curing. Salt of sufficient quality was imported from Brittany and Spain but the import tax rose to forty times the value of the salt itself.

The tax on tea rose to 110%, and there were eighteen different duties on brandy and gin, totalling around 250%. The tax burden on the ordinary population was enormous. Against this background Cornish people generally had no qualms about turning to smuggling to survive and support their families.

The popular romantic myth portrays Cornish smugglers as colourful pirates.

Salt and other goods subject to these massive tax hikes were a fraction of the price in France and the Channel Islands, only one or two days sailing. Therefore with their expert maritime skills, it is no surprise Cornish fishermen became adept smugglers.

The popular perception of Cornish smugglers is of bands of rough men armed with cutlasses and flintlock pistols and dressed as colourful pirates. The reality is more mundane. Real Cornish smugglers came from the ranks of hard-working fishermen and poor agricultural labourers. However, by the 1780s, what had begun as an impoverished people struggling to survive, quickly grew into a much bigger enterprise with the general realisation large fortunes could be made.

Real Cornish smugglers came from the ranks of hard-working fishermen and poor agricultural labourers.

Free Trade

The scene was set for a smuggling explosion, or as the locals called it 'Cornish Free Trade'. With a clear run from the southern coast of Cornwall, the island of Guernsey and the French port of Roscoff became the main source of contraband supply enabling Cornwall to develop into one of the principal centres of free trade in Britain.

Merchants in the Channel Islands and Northern France specifically packaged the goods for English smugglers. Special 4½ gallon 'half-anker' barrels were manufactured with ropes or harnesses conveniently attached, allowing easier carrying as two tubs could weigh as much as a hundredweight. Goods like tobacco and tea were wrapped in oilskin coverings to prevent contact with sea water during the crossing.

Contraband landed in Cornish coves was ferried by rowboats from sailing ships anchored offshore.

Initially, smuggling took place fairly openly with cargoes landed directly on the shore, made possible by the involvement of all sections of the community, from the local landowner downwards.

A typical consignment consisted of 500 half-anker tubs of brandy, Geneva (gin) or rum. Smugglers' sailing luggers arriving back on the Cornish coast were too large to come in close to the rocky landing sites. Instead they anchored offshore, allowing smaller boats to be rowed out to collect as many barrels as possible. Men and horses stood by on the beaches to transport the contraband inland.

Opposite: 'Tub men' often carried two half-anker casks using rope slings attached by the Guernsey merchants.
(Courtesy of St Barbe Museum)

When smugglers feared attack by the Revenue Services they engaged 'batmen' armed with weighted sticks for protection. Mullion historian Reverend E. G. Harvey, writing in 1875, maintained that violence involving bloodshed was less frequent in Cornwall than Kent where smugglers were organised into large gangs capable of great violence if they were confronted by men of the Preventive Services.

'Batmen' with weighted sticks protected contraband carriers from attack by Preventive forces.

Eager Customers

Most contraband landed in Cornwall was distributed for local consumption with publicans and innkeepers as an essential part of the chain. Members of the gentry were also some of the best customers as were clergymen. Rectory dining tables were well laden with fine wines and good brandy. Church curates, with the advantage of being literate and numerate,

Cornwall is littered with relics of former tin and copper mines worked by thirsty customers of the free traders.

were known to have been employed as smugglers' book-keepers.

Some of the landed free trade goods were destined for customers further inland. Helston became a distribution centre forwarding contraband goods up country. Large quantities of spirits were despatched to the thirsty, hard-working tin miners, particularly around the areas of Camborne and Redruth.

A percentage of the goods landed at Falmouth was conveyed north across the windswept wastes of Bodmin Moor bound for Jamaica Inn and beyond. It was once estimated that if all the goods smuggled through Falmouth alone in the course of one year had been taxed, the collected revenue would have been more than double the land tax for the whole kingdom.

The Financiers

Smuggling runs in Cornwall were sometimes financed by small groups of people from individual fishing villages. At other times wealthy farmers like Dionysius Williams and Christopher Pollard from Sennen organised and financed complete runs which included dealing with merchants, paying sailors, organising landing parties and transacting with customers. It helped that these two entrepreneurs also owned pubs.

Members of the gentry, including politicians and magistrates were also known to be financial backers. In 1750, the Mayor of Penzance was bound over *'not to be again guilty of smuggling'*. The participation of the gentry ranged from turning a blind eye, to full scale involvement. The wealth and influence of the Killigrew family, who established Falmouth, derived from smuggling and piracy.

Winter Storms and Wrecking

Wrecking, or more accurately 'plundering', has gone on ever since ships began to sail the seas. The fact that the wreckers of Cornwall gained more notoriety than those elsewhere was because more ships fell prey to the savage winter storms and dangerous rocky coastline.

Tobias Smollett, in his *New History of England* published in 1758, described wrecking as: *'One of the most notorious eighteenth-century crimes receiving the sanction of the entire local community'*.

Certain legends led people to believe ships were deliberately lured into danger by a display of false lights and survivors callously murdered, so there would be no witnesses to the heinous crime. This is really a slur on seafaring smuggling communities. The truth is such subterfuge simply would not

work. Mariners interpret a light on land as a warning to keep a safe distance.

Opposite: A recent ferocious storm at Sennen with *The Old Success Inn* in the foreground.

Moreover, oil lanterns cannot be seen any distance over water at night, unless they are large, fitted with mirrors or lenses, and mounted at a great height (i.e. in a lighthouse). No surviving captain of a wrecked ship ever charged he had been led astray by a false light. Smugglers necessarily were expert mariners, with the greatest respect for the sea and sympathy for those who found themselves in peril. Early lifeboat crews would have been smugglers to a man.

The notorious Mount's Bay wreckers at work on the remnants of a vessel near St Michael's Mount.

There is no recorded instance of deliberate wrecking and the inhumane murder of survivors, while 'plundering' is an entirely different matter. Wrecked vessels along the south Cornish coast were considered to be 'God given' and the goods and materials they provided viewed as precious and necessary bounty to alleviate the harsh and meagre existence of coast dwellers.

The Preventive Services

Throughout most of the free trade era Cornish smugglers had the upper hand over the Preventive Services. Cornwall's terrain favoured smuggling with its long expanses of rocky, virtually uninhabited coast. With few patrolling Revenue Men to police the situation smuggling rose to epidemic proportions.

With a great many able bodied men away at war the Preventive Service was frequently undermanned. Those who did take the lonely job of Riding Officer were principally recruited from ex-cavalry men. Although some were gallant and

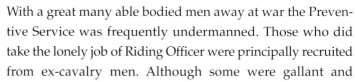

Customs' Riding Officers patrolled the coast at night but were generally ineffectual at combatting smuggling.

honest, they were continually criticised and many were open to bribery. Lax supervision permitted some to retain their jobs (and the pay attached) until they were eighty years old and beyond chasing smugglers.

However, from around 1800 Revenue Men became more organised and proactive. Smuggled goods had to be dropped off in remote coves, and picked up again when the coast was clear. Tunnels and passages were dug out of the rocks to expedite movement. After 1831 Coastguards became more vigilant

Coastguards 'creeping' with grappling irons to retrieve sunken contraband.

and the old fashioned 'runs' became ineffectual. Contraband was weighted and sunk close inshore to be collected later. The coastguards business was to find it by 'creeping' with grappling irons and claim the prize money.

It was earlier in 1700 when Revenue Authorities struck on the obvious plan of pursuing smugglers at sea. At first this met with little success since they hired coasters and fishing-smacks whose crews were generally smugglers themselves. The original luggers owned by the smuggling communities were built solely for fishing but, as the activity progressed and free trade money increased, some smugglers commissioned fast, purpose-built contraband carrying vessels.

Things had changed by the early nineteenth century with Revenue Cutters having become very fine ships with a tall single mast. Often the government wisely employed shipyards famous for building speedy smugglers' luggers. Prize money was always the incentive and some cutters with their huge sails were very fast and sufficiently well-armed to tackle any smuggler.

A Customs Cutter in hot pursuit of a smugglers' lugger.

The End of an Era

After the Battle of Waterloo in 1815 the attention of the armed services was directed to combating domestic smuggling. In 1817 the Royal Navy began highly successful blockade techniques and in 1831 The Coastguard Service was formed becoming part of the Royal Navy.

Coastguards were eventually stationed all along the coast and terraces of Coastguards' cottages are still a familiar sight. This initiative, together with a gradual reduction in taxation on smugglers' favoured goods, saw the decline and eventual demise of the 'Golden Age' of smuggling.

Sennen Coastguard Cottages circa 1893, home to the extended families of Chief Officer Thomas Stone and his five men.

The risks of apprehension and prosecution became higher. Serious trials were conducted outside the county because Cornish juries would not convict smugglers. Offenders were jailed and those implicated in violence could be sentenced to death or, if they were lucky, to transportation to colonies such as Australia. Robert Lang, a smuggler from Veryan is recorded as being hanged at the crossroads of Ruan Lanihorne and St Mawes as an example to others.

John Wesley's Crusade

Methodist John Wesley preached against the evils of smuggling and wrecking.

John Wesley visited Cornwall on more than thirty occasions bringing the message of Methodism and decrying the evils of smuggling and, in particular, wrecking. On Saturday 17 August 1775 he made the following entry in his journal:

We found Mr. Hoskins, at Cubert, alive, but just tottering over the grave. I preached in the evening on II Corinthians 5:1-4, probably the last sermon he will hear from me. I was afterward inquiring if that scandal of Cornwall, the plundering of wrecked vessels, still subsisted. He said, "As much as ever; only the Methodists will have nothing to do with it. But three months since a vessel was wrecked on the south coast, and the tinners presently seized on all the goods and even broke in pieces a new coach which was on board and carried every scrap of it away."

But is there no way to prevent this shameful breach of all the laws both of religion and humanity? Indeed there is. The gentry of Cornwall may totally prevent it whenever they please. Let them only see that the laws be strictly executed upon the next plunderers; and after an example is made of ten of these, the next wreck will be unmolested. Nay, there is a milder way. Let them only agree together to discharge any tinner or laborer that is concerned in the plundering of a wreck and advertise his name that no Cornish gentleman may employ him anymore; and neither tinner nor laborer will any more be concerned in that bad work'.

It is said that Wesley's influence greatly helped to bring an end to the free trade but simple economics played a greater part. When Prime Minister William Pitt significantly reduced the rate of duty on luxury goods the risks involved in smuggling were no longer worth taking.

Smugglers' Pubs

There were occasional pockets of smuggling on the north coast of Cornwall but the main activity took place along the south coast. The most common destinations for contraband

This photograph of a Methodist meeting at Gwennap Pit in 1907 evokes a sense of what it must have been like in Wesley's time.

One of the hundreds of beer houses or' kiddly-winks' scattered throughout Cornwall in earlier centuries.

were the pubs and inns where goods could be sampled, stored and, of course, sold. Smugglers themselves often frequented 'kiddlywinks' or beer houses where customers in the know would wink at the landlord or landlady and be served some 'under the counter' spirits.

In all the southern counties of England the nerve centre of smuggling operations was predominantly the local pub. Here plots were hatched, arrangements for transportation agreed and runs commissioned. The smugglers' pub served as a meeting place, recruitment centre, secret storage facility, distribution depot and valued customer.

This book is a journey of discovery round Cornwall's southern coast from Penzance all the way to Falmouth. It is a guide to a significant number of authentic pubs patronised over two centuries ago by Cornish smugglers. These wonderful old buildings with low-beamed ceilings, flagstone floors, inglenook fireplaces and secret hiding places are where, with a little imagination, one can sense the desperate days of the free traders.

The local pub was the smugglers' headquarters where plots were hatched, arrangements for transportation agreed and runs commissioned.

(Courtesy of Buckler's Hard Maritime Museum)

Standing right on the harbourside and frequented by generations of seafaring smugglers, The Sloop Inn is understandably a magnet for tourists.

St Ives
The Sloop Inn
The Wharf, St Ives TR26 1LP

Tel: 01736 796584

www.sloop-inn.co.uk

St Ives Bay is the first inlet north of Land's End that is shel-tered from Atlantic storms. With five sandy beaches, pictur-esque harbour and maze of narrow streets this former fishing and mining centre still retains a special atmosphere despite the swarm of summer visitors.

Throughout the eighteenth century the windows of The Sloop looked out on a thriving smuggling scene. John Wesley, who with his brother Charles founded the Methodist Movement, visited Cornwall thirty-two times between 1743 and 1791. In September 1757 he visited St Ives and left us this impression with its mistaken conclusion:

Adnams Ghost Ship and Dart-moor Jail Ale are complemented by Sharp's Doom Bar, a truly local beer brewed at Rock, a few miles up the north Cornish coast.

On Wednesday, 25, the stewards met at St. Ives, from the western part of Cornwall. The next day I began examining the society, but I was soon obliged to stop short. I found an accursed thing among them; well-nigh one and all bought or sold uncustomed goods. I therefore delayed speaking to any more till I had met them all together. This I did in the evening and told them plainly either they must put this abomination away or they would see my face no more. Friday, 27. They severally promised so to do. So I trust this plague is stayed.

Slate floors, black beamed ceilings and nautical artefacts engender a true sense of history in this 700-year-old smugglers' pub.

In the bars, 'St Ives' School' drawings decorate the walls.

In the smoky atmosphere of the Sloop's black-beamed bars free traders exchanged information on smuggling runs and swapped tales of personalities like John Knill, Collector of Customs from 1762 to 1782 and Mayor of the borough from 1767 to 1782. Knill was in league with the squire of Trevetho, and was known to have paid for the fitting out of a privateer used as a smuggling vessel. He also built a 50 foot high granite obelisk on Worvas Hill which appears to be a folly but served a useful purpose as a sea-mark for Knill's vessels.

In his will the former smuggling mayor left money for the upkeep of his obelisk and for celebrations to take place every five years on St James's Day, 25 July. This involves the majority of the townsfolk and is an occasion for a good deal of jollity. Ten young virgins and two widows, accompanied by a fiddle player, dance around the obelisk whilst spectators sing Psalm 100, '*Make a joyful noise unto the Lord all ye lands*'. The vicar and current mayor also waltz sedately around on the upper step of the monument, hand in hand with the girls.

John Knill's obelisk where, on 25 July at five-yearly intervals, two widows and ten young virgins dance while townsfolk sing Psalm 100.

During the eighteenth century huge quantities of contraband were landed openly on the beach immediately in front of the pub.

Throughout the eighteenth century the windows of The Sloop looked out on a thriving smuggling scene.

Another notorious frequenter of The Sloop Inn was James 'Old Worm' Williams who, on one occasion, landed smuggled Irish whiskey close to St Ives breakwater and hid the barrels in fishing boats and pigsties. Later that night, three carts collected the contraband and carried it openly through the streets heading east towards Hayle. The noise of the convoy attracted the attention of a Coastguard drinking in the George & Dragon in the market place. When he went to investigate he was knocked to the ground, bound and gagged.

Finally escaping, the Coastguard enlisted the help of a Riding Officer who galloped to the tollhouse on Hayle causeway. The toll keeper denied seeing any wagons but in truth the smugglers had acquired new horses and continued their journey north. The Riding Officer concluded they had headed south for Penzance and consequently made a fruitless trip in the wrong direction.

The *St George*, Williams' smack, was still in the bay with only the Prussian cabin-boy on board. Nicknamed 'Prussian Bob', the lad eventually settled in St Ives and became known as 'Old Worm's Fool' on account of his fine performance on that night, pretending to understand only three words of English: '*I don't know*'.

On 4 December 1815 the London Custom House issued the following notice:

Whereas it has been represented to the Commissioners of His Majesty's Customs, that in the night of the 23rd day of Novem-

ber last, *Richard Hosking, sitter of the preventive boat in the service of the Customs, stationed at the port of St. Ives, in the county of Cornwall, seized on shore within the said port, between two hundred and three hundred casks of smuggled spirits; after which, the said Richard Hosking and his assistants were violently assaulted, and obstructed by a great number of smugglers unknown, who rescued and carried away the said goods'.*

'The Commissioners of His Majesty's Customs, in order to bring the offenders to justice, are hereby pleased to offer a reward of £200 to any person or persons who shall discover and apprehend, or cause to be discovered and apprehended, any one or more of the said offenders, to be paid by the Collector of Customs at the port of St. Ives, upon conviction'.

In St Ives a variation on traditional Cornish smuggling practices took place. Fishermen rowed out to meet slave ships
returning from the West Indies to Bristol with cargoes of rum

St Nicholas Chapel perched
on the hill overlooking St
Ives Bay was used by
Customs men as a lookout
for smugglers.

Men and pack ponies laden with contraband made their way through the narrow cobbled streets.

and sugar. These luxuries were then made available throughout West Cornwall and Bristol merchants even came to St Ives to buy duty free sugar.

Dated to circa 1312, this ancient hostelry is situated right on the harbour front with only a cobbled fore-court and road separating it from the sea. One of the oldest and most famous pubs in Cornwall, The Sloop Inn is a favourite haunt of locals, fishermen, artists and tourists all year round.

Outside seating on the cobbles affords wonderful beach and harbour views. 'St Ives' School' drawings are displayed inside the busy, low-beamed, panelled and flagstoned rooms. Most of the comfortably appointed bedrooms overlook the pretty bay.

There is good value food from sandwiches to interesting baguettes, with the main meal menu majoring on local seafood from line-caught St Ives Bay mackerel to home-made fishcakes of Newlyn cod and smoked haddock. Adnams Ghost Ship and Dartmoor Jail Ale are complemented by Sharp's Doom Bar, a truly local beer brewed at Rock, a few miles up the north Cornish coast.

St Just
The Star Inn
1 Fore Street, St Just TR19 7LL

Tel: 01736 788767

www.thestarinn-stjust.co.uk

The Star Inn at St Just is a true gem, full of tradition, character and immense charm.

St Just stands at the southwestern margin of one of the most remarkable areas of industrial archaeology in the country. This austere community of low granite houses and inns was once an important tin and copper mining centre.

Smuggling in Cornwall before 1805 was an open practice. Ships called at Guernsey where spirits were legally purchased in large barrels. During the return passage the contents were

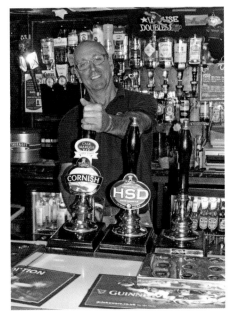

transferred to tubs which were landed and distributed. Later authorities more effectively intercepted contraband runs and increasingly smugglers became reliant on guile rather than force. Most cargoes were sunk offshore for later retrieval and more remote shores like that at St Just were increasingly used.

Thomas Hicks, one of the innkeepers of St Just, set off in an open boat with seven crew and £100 in bank notes and bills. He had collected the money to purchase goods from a lugger lying offshore at Priest's Cove. When returning with the contraband his boat capsized in the heavy surf and he and four of the crew drowned. On a later occasion spirits and tobacco were found concealed in mine workings

Jonney McFadden runs a 'proper pub' appreciated by local beer drinking enthusiasts and visitors alike. When I enquired about food he said: 'We have crisps!'

Dark walls in the dimly lit bar are decorated with photographs and maritime memorabilia whilst flags from all nations cover the ceilings.

The rooms in this friendly local are separated by a passage that leads from the front door to the original stable yard.

at St Just and on a subsequent search one of the preventive men fell down a shaft to his death.

Around 1818 two smugglers from St Just, Oats and Perme-wan, were very active in the area. They took the precaution of employing a middleman/banker called Pridham who paid the merchants in France for the goods smuggled into Britain.

However, it appears Pridham became greedy, and kept more than his agreed percentage. He also threatened to report the smugglers to the authorities if they failed to comply with the new arrangement. A meeting was set to discuss the terms of the contract and to avoid potential prosecution based on Pridham's evidence. Oats and Permewan hatched a plan based on the fact Pridham had only met Permewan in person a couple of times. Permewan sent his brother to impersonate him and while the meeting took place, Permewan himself established the perfect alibi by meeting as many people in the town as possible – which no doubt meant visiting The Star.

Opposite: The Star's lunchtime 'suppers' club' where the entertainment is essentially conversation and the locals are always ready to spin a yarn or two!

This brilliant design of a suspended sail provides year round protection cover for alfresco drinkers.

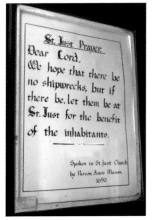

St. Just Prayer.
Dear Lord.
We hope that there be
no shipwrecks, but if
there be, let them be at
St. Just for the benefit
of the inhabitants.

Spoken in St Just Church
by Parson Amos Mason
1650

Reverend Amos Mason would have known that all poverty-stricken communities around Cornwall's rugged coast subscribed to this sad philosophy.

When the blackmailer eventually made his accusations his evidence was ruled out of court.

Full of tradition, character and immense charm this ancient pub is a true gem which has featured in several television and film roles. To enter is to step back in time. It is run by friendly landlord Jonney McFadden and his wife Julia and is much appreciated by local beer drinking aficionados and visitors alike. The Star is a 'proper pub', one of the few left in the country that sell only wines, spirits and, of course, well-kept beer! No food is served but patrons are very welcome to take in their own sandwiches.

Day time entertainment is essentially conversation and locals are always ready to spin a yarn or two! In the evening traditional pub games are played in the low-beamed, spick-and-span bar which is the hub of the local folk scene, with live

This very early example of flash photography provides a glimpse of the working conditions endured by the tin miners of St Just.

music at least ten nights every month. Singalongs and joke-telling are part of the Monday evening gatherings.

The dimly-lit bar is jam-packed with interest and the walls are scattered with seafaring and mining artefacts. Coals glow in the grate on wild winter days when mulled wine is served and there is an all-weather covered courtyard.

Sennen Cove
The Old Success Inn

Cove Hill, Sennen Cove TR19 7DG

Tel: 01736 871232

www.oldsuccess.co.uk

The Old Success Inn has seventeenth-century origins.

Sennen Cove situated at the end of a spur road, is approximately a mile from Land's End. The Cove lies at the southern end of Whitesand Bay whose sandy beaches extend further north along the coast towards the Cape Cornwall peninsula; England's only cape. With clear blue sea and fine sands, Sennen Cove is a breathtakingly beautiful location. Regarded as one of Britain's best beaches and known by many as the bay where dolphins play.

The Old Success enjoys
views from Sennen Cove
across Whitesand Bay.

In the nineteenth century pilchards and red mullet were not the only items landed at Sennen Cove. The beach was regularly used for landing contraband and smuggling was controlled and financed by wealthy farmer Christopher Pollard from Madron. In 1803 Pollard was living in Guernsey where he had fled to escape imprisonment on a smuggling charge.

The original inn known by smugglers prior to 1922.

The island of Guernsey had become a refuge for Cornish smugglers wanted by the law but by now forces of the Crown were once again involved in fighting the Napoleonic Wars

and needed men for the services and home defence. A Royal Proclamation was made that any smuggler living in exile, but not charged with murder, be permitted to return without fear of arrest, on entering into a bond to refrain from smuggling practices for the future.

This 1691 etched date stone can be seen in the staircase wall leading from the dining room.

Copies of this proclamation were posted in all Cornish villages and it was not long before the news filtered through to those who were lying in exile overseas. Pollard was among the first to take advantage of the amnesty. Returning to Cornwall he signed the requisite bond, with Robert Parsons of Madron standing surety for the sum of £200.

However, by 1805, Pollard was again charged with smuggling. The prosecution states that on this occasion the accused had assaulted Officers of H.M. Excise when occupied in their duty at Sennen, and incited a crowd of three or four hundred persons to attack the Excisemen with a view to carrying off the smuggled goods which they had captured and were defending on the beach.

The landing was indeed a valuable one, consisting of one thousand gallons of brandy, one thousand gallons of rum, one thousand gallons of Geneva, and five hundred pounds of tobacco. In addition to the general charge of inciting the mob, Pollard was accused of having offered £100 for the rescue of a hundred ankers of the spirits and *'of using other violent and improper language'*.

The main witness for the prosecution was Annie George, landlady of the Sennen Churchtown Inn who by this time was

Light and airy in summer, the log fire ensures the Old Success bar is cosy in winter. The artist's poster over the fireplace acknowledges the inn as the focal point of the Sennen Lifeboat Crew.

generally regarded as a malicious gossip. A. K. Hamilton Jenkin in *Cornwall and its People* states that: *'no less than five people have been capitally indicted by her means one of whom had already been executed'*. The case against Pollard was dismissed and he was acquitted but subsequently imprisoned for smuggling off Plymouth.

Opposite: The varying floor levels and the thickness of the walls give a clue to the inn's antiquity.

Deep set windows look out across Whitesand Bay to The Brisons rocks and Cape Cornwall.

Enjoying magnificent views across Whitesand Bay towards The Brisons rocks and Cape Cornwall, The Old Success Inn looks the least likely building to be a smugglers' pub but it conceals a secret – there is an original historic inn at its heart. The date 1691 can be seen etched into exposed stonework on the wall of a staircase leading up from the restaurant.

The present Old Success has developed from a seventeenth-century fishermen's and smugglers' inn. Over the years, it has been extended and modernised and now comprises a bar, restaurant, residents' lounge, twelve en-suite bedrooms and three self-catering apartments plus a raised sea-facing terrace.

The raised sea-facing terrace provides perfect opportunities for alfresco drinking and dining.

The original inn had just three bars: the jug and bottle at the back (just big enough for access), plus the saloon and finally the 'Top Room'. Everything changed in 1922 when great swathes of Sennen property were sold off. Ernest Barton, the inn's new owner, converted it, adding another storey and renamed it the Whitesand Bay Hotel. Decades of further development and modernisation followed although it has reverted now to its original name.

Hearty food is served all year round with fresh local seafood to the fore with favourites including Tribute battered catch of the day and Cornish fish pie. Non-fishy choices include Cajun-style chicken, goat's cheese tart, Cornish pasty with chips and casserole of the day. The St Austell's beer range has seasonal variations such as the amber coloured 'Ruck & Roll' rugby-themed ale with a full dry palate balanced by fruity hops.

The magnificent beach at Whitesand Bay where, in 1805, three-hundred or more men attacked Revenue Officers guarding a huge cache of contraband.

Sennen Churchtown
The First & Last Inn
Land's End, Sennen, Penzance TR19 7AA

Tel: 01736 871680

www.firstandlastinn.co.uk

The First & Last at Sennen Church-town now comprises two adjoining build-ings.

While England's northwest coast is being eroded at an alarming rate the granite rocks of Land's End peninsula continue to withstand the Atlantic surges. Arthur Mee in his book on Cornwall, in the county series *The King's England* wrote of Land's End: '*The very idea of standing at the end of our sea-girt isle may bring a touch of wonder into the dullest mind. It is the farthest outreach into the restless sea of the home of a great sea race.*'

The old inn as the smugglers would have known it.

John Wesley visited this bare bleak peninsula in 1744 and, inspired by the rugged landscape, wrote the poem beginning: '*Lo! on a narrow neck of land, Twixt two unbounded seas I stand*'. At this time Sennen was a centre for

CIRCA 1620

THE ENTRANCE TO
SMUGGLERS TUNNEL
RUNNING TO THE CLIFFS

ANNIE'S WELL

Former landlady Ann Treeve presided
over smuggling and wrecking operations
together with the local parson, until
turning Queen's evidence against Dionysius
Williams a Sennen farmer (the smuggling
agent) who then served a long prison
sentence. For Annie's 'service' to the crown
she was staked out on Sennen Beach and
drowned by the incoming tide. Her body
was laid out in the large upstairs room in
this inn prior to the burial in an unmarked
grave, for fear of retribution by way of
grave robbers.

PLEASE DON'T STEP ON THE GLASS

Annie's Well, now covered over with glass, is located in a passage leading through to the original part of the pub. *Left: 'Why spoil a good story with too many facts?'*

smuggling with landings taking place a couple of miles north at Whitesand Bay, while the inhospitable rocky coast at Land's End lent itself more to shipwrecks and opportunities for plunder.

There are two pubs at Sennen; this at Churchtown, close to Land's End, is now known as 'The First & Last'. The other is located at nearby Sennen Cove known now as 'The Old Success' and is featured in the previous entry. Confusingly,

The original part of the inn still retains low ceilings and some exposed brick walls.

The main dining room is light and airy with white walls and large windows.

both establishments historically have been referred to simply as The Inn at Sennen.

Around the beginning of the nineteenth century both pubs were individually owned by well-to-do local farmers. The First & Last was the property of Dionysius Williams while Christopher Pollard owned the land and The Old Success Inn at the cove. Both men funded and controlled local smuggling operations. Pollard's landlord at the Cove Inn was fisherman Mathew George while Mathew's brother Joseph ran this inn at Churchtown with his wife Ann; known as Annie.

The former stable yard has been transformed into a sheltered beer garden.

Annie George (née Treeves) is the villain of this story. Her husband Joseph was smuggling agent for their landlord, the pub's owner Dionysius Williams. Annie used her knowledge of Williams' smuggling activities to blackmail him into letting the two of them live rent-free at the inn. Williams called her bluff and the couple were

evicted. This infuriated Annie and she turned King's Evidence against him, after receiving immunity from prosecution for herself and Joseph. Some accounts say Dionysius served a long term of imprisonment but this seems unlikely as a Cornish jury would never have convicted him. It is more likely he escaped to the Channel Islands.

In the floor of the passage leading through to the bar is a glass-covered well with a notice stating: THE ENTRANCE TO SMUGGLERS TUNNEL RUNNING TO THE CLIFFS. This bit of fun with a tunnel, a local parson, a gruesome slow death and grave diggers makes interesting reading for tourists but is not confirmed by known facts.

There are documented incidents of smugglers whipping informers but no accounts of elaborate drownings as described on the information board. Annie could not have turned 'Queen's Evidence' in 1802 because King George III was the reigning monarch and digging tunnels through granite also seems unlikely. All this comes under the category of: *'Why spoil a good story with too many facts?'*

However, Annie did exist and in another legal brief in 1805, she turned King's Evidence against Christopher Pollard, accusing him of landing a very valuable cargo at Sennen Cove, a story featured in the previous chapter.

The photographs show how the original single storey inn has developed over the centuries with the addition of a second floor and a large adjoining building. The First & Last is foremost a tourist attraction and worth a visit for its location alone. There is live music on Saturday nights, a sheltered beer garden and log fires for winter days and nights.

Lamorna
Lamorna Wink

Near Penzance TR19 6XQ

Tel: 01736 731566

www.lamornawink.co

The early eighteenth-century granite pub was a haunt for smugglers who landed contraband at the cove.

Lamorna is an isolated hamlet set in a craggy granite cove at the end of a beautiful wooded valley. A narrow lane leads from the Lamorna Wink pub to the cove car park and quay below. The small village is half a mile inland.

In the late nineteenth and early twentieth centuries Lamorna became popular with artists of the Newlyn School and is particularly associated with Samuel John 'Lamorna' Birch who lived there from 1908 and the flamboyant, hard drinking Alfred Munnings, later knighted and considered by many to be the finest English painter of horses. He was a friend of Major General J. E. B. Seely, whose account of his war horse Warrior perhaps inspired the highly acclaimed novel by Michael Morpurgo *War Horse*, now made into a film.

Munnings lost the sight of his right eye in an accident when he was twenty (a blow from a briar when lifting a dog over a hedge) and, as a result, was rejected by the Army. He spent much of the first three years of World War One at Lamorna producing some superb paintings including 'The Wink' for Mr Jory the landlord to offset his bar bill.

A 'Wink' was the name for a Cornish ale house where customers in the know would wink at the 'brandy' kettle when they desired something stronger than beer.

He concentrated on the people and animals, not bothering with the detail of the pub's stonework but was careful to include Jory's name over the door. He later went to France as a war artist and painted Major General Seely mounted on Warrior. The session was temporarily halted when they came under artillery fire.

In 1901 Frank Heath moved to Newlyn to study with Stanhope Forbes and left an evocative interior scene painted in the Wink at that time. This period is dramatised in the 1998

Sir Alfred Munnings (1878 – 1959) was one of England's finest painters of horses. He produced this painting of the pub during the First World War when it was owned by Mr. Jory.
(© Estate of Sir Alfred Munnings. All rights reserved DACS)

novel *Summer in February* by Jonathan Smith and adapted for
the 2013 film directed by Christopher Menaul.

Spoil tips on the eastern side of the cove are a reminder of the
Lamorna Granite Quarries, first opened by John Freeman in
1849 and continued working until 1911. The Freeman family
exported stone to London for the construction of Westminster
embankment. The rugged beauty is captured in the 1929
poem *Lamorna Cove* by 'super-tramp' W. H. Davies:

> *I SEE at last our great Lamorna Cove,*
> *Which, danced on by ten thousand silver feet,*
> *Has all those waves that run like little lambs,*
> *To draw the milk from many a rocky teat,*
> *Spilt in white gallons all along the shore.*
> *Who ever saw more beauty under the sun?*

Set among granite cliffs at the western
side of Mounts Bay, Lamorna Cove
was a favourite landing beach for
smugglers. The late eighteenth-
century Lamorna Wink Inn stands at
the head of the smugglers' trail,
leading up from the Cove. Local free
traders concealed their contraband in
a hiding place under the floor in front
of the fireplace.

The smart dining
area has a cosy
corner by the
wood burning
stove for the
cooler days and
evenings.

The 'Wink' part of the pub's name comes from kiddlywink
(sometimes spelt kiddleywink), an old name for a Cornish
beer shop or beer house, which became popular after the 1830
beer act. They were licensed to sell beer or cider by Customs
& Excise rather than by a Magistrate's Licence which was
required for traditional public houses and inns.

Wink taverns were haunts of smugglers and landlords or landladies would use a kettle to keep smuggled brandy hidden from the law. Customers in the know would wink at the kettle when they desired something stronger than beer.

A decade ago the Lamorna Wink was scruffy and cluttered with maritime and other artefacts on walls and ceilings. It was delightful and full of character but has since changed to satisfy the requirements of modern families. It received a complete interior face-lift and is now bright, smart and clean. Luckily all of the important collection of naval artefacts has been retained including the nameplate of the battleship *Warspite*.

With many Cornish pubs being tied to a brewery it is a welcome change to discover a free house. Among the varying

Opposite: Apart from exposed stone on some walls the Wink today has a completely modern interior.

Inset: The Wink is a free house offering a varying selection of interesting ales.

Today this important collection of maritime artefacts is displayed to good effect.

ales on offer at the Wink is 'Nice Try', a copper-coloured beer, with a light malty aroma and a pleasing sharp bitter tang. Brewed by Bays, a family-run business based in Torbay, Devon, this ale has the strength of character to complement tasty dishes like stews, hard cheeses and meat-packed pasties. Betty Stoggs, named after a famous character from Cornish folklore and brewed by Skinners, is a favourite, smooth, amber ale found throughout Cornwall.

The rugged beauty of the cove inspired generations of artists and writers. Spoil tips on the eastern side are a reminder of granite quarries first opened by John Freeman in 1849 which continued working until 1911.

Mousehole
The Ship Inn
South Cliff, Mousehole TR19 6QX

Tel: 01736 731234

www.shipinnmousehole.co.uk

Set right on the water's edge in the safe haven of Mousehole, The Ship Inn is a perfect spot for observing the harbour's marine activity.

Mousehole, 2 miles south of Penzance, is the archetypal Cornish village. Cottages once occupied by fishermen and smugglers progress charmingly down the steep hillside to the waters' edge where they cluster around one of the most beautiful harbours in Britain. The name Mousehole, pronounced 'Mauzl', possibly derives from the Cornish 'mouz bel, or maiden's brook.

Surprisingly, this tranquil place has a violent history. It was invaded by a Spanish raiding party in July 1595, during the

course of which the whole village, save one house, was burnt down. When the settlement was reconstructed the cottages were built of granite. The house which survived the holocaust was that of Squire Jenkyn Keigwin, who tragically was killed while defending it. The Elizabethan manor house, distinguished by a porch of granite columns, still stands to the present day.

Opposite: Through the harbour entrance St Michael's Mount can be seen rising majestically above the waters of the bay.

Mousehole is the most westerly of Mount Bay's smuggling villages. In 1700 it was the place where pilgrims embarked for the Holy Land and was a much more important fishing port than Newlyn. Ships from Mousehole carried pilchards to France and the Mediterranean, and returned with salt needed in their processing, much smuggled in without payment of duty.

This plaque pays tribute to Charles Greenhaugh, landlord of The Ship in 1981, and to the remainder of the lifeboat crew, all lost at sea in a December storm.

In the mid eighteenth century the Collector and his staff from Penzance Customs House were responsible for 35 miles of

Left: The flagstone floor and black beams lend atmosphere to the old bar. *Above:* This snug little corner would have witnessed many a hushed conversation about contraband landings.

coastline which included the village of Mousehole. In 1740, in response to his desperate pleas for military help in the battle against smugglers, he was allocated three officers and 25 privates, only two being assigned to Mousehole.

When the soldiers were later withdrawn contraband was again carried openly during the day through the narrow winding streets. Writing in 1775, George Borlase author of *The Natural History of Cornwall* lamented:

> *The coasts here swarm with smugglers from land's End to the lizard ... so I wonder the soldiers should have been ordered off without being replaced by others.*

When the Preventive Officer assigned to Mousehole was asked why he had not apprehended the smugglers he said he had been pelted with stones, and lay in his bed recovering.

The names of individual smugglers, who would certainly have been regulars at The Ship, are listed in Custom House

Left: The pubby food selection served in the dining room includes fine local fish dishes. *Above:* On the wall behind these happy customers are photographs of some of the ferocious winter storms encountered at Mousehole.

records. In 1757 William Allen Cutler and William Keigwin, both of Mousehole, were convicted of smuggling. In 1771 Richard Pentreath (alias 'Doga'), was convicted of smuggling and described by the Penzance Collector of Customs as 'an honest man in all his dealings though a notorious smuggler'. At the same time, Thomas Mann, another convicted Mousehole smuggler, was also described as honest.

The 'Cask Marque' label on the beer pumps is an independent award for pubs serving quality cask ale.

The following year, Richard Mann and John Thomas were convicted, while in 1776 all the Customs Men in Mousehole were charged with accepting bribes and actively assisting in smuggling. In 1792, in the narrow lane leading up to the

Smugglers moved contraband openly through the narrow streets which today are a blaze of colour from fuchsias, hydrangeas and geraniums flourishing in the temperate climate. *Right:* Squire Jenkyn Keigwin forfeited his life saving this building during the 1595 Spanish attack on the village.

nearby village of Paul, Martha Blewett was murdered for money she made selling untaxed salt.

Set right on the water's edge in the safe haven of Mousehole, The Ship is a perfect spot for observing the harbour's marine activity and for absorbing the unique atmosphere of this bustling community.

The Ship is a traditional Cornish inn, with a sun-bleached granite and slate exterior, slate floors, low ceilings and a warm welcome. The dimly lit main bar has black beams, flag-stones and an open fire. The walls are part panelled with built-in wooden benches and stools around low tables.

In terms of temperature, appearance, aroma and taste The Ship's well-kept St Austell ales have received the independent 'Cask Marque' accreditation and the pubby food selection includes good local fish. There is a separate restaurant and affordable accommodation with eight stylish bedrooms.

In 1792, in the narrow lane leading up to the nearby village of Paul, Martha Blewett was murdered for money she made selling untaxed salt.

The Tolcarne Inn is a traditional seventeenth-century quayside pub.

Newlyn
Tolcarne Inn

Tolcarne Place, Newlyn TR18 5PR

Tel: 01736 363074

www.tolcarneinn.co.uk

Newlyn is the largest fishing port in the southwest of England and its economy is largely dependent on its harbour and the associated fishing industry. Tolcarne (Tal Carn: Brow of the Rocks) is one of three hamlets, originally separated by water, that comprise present day Newlyn. Lying on the western shore of Mounts Bay it forms a conurbation with neighbouring Penzance and is the southernmost town on the British mainland – though not the most southerly settlement.

The hamlet of Tolcarne was originally separated by water from the main part of the town.

While superb food prepared by the chef-landlord is the priority at the Tolcarne Inn one may nevertheless just pop in for a pint.

In the 1880s a number of artists flocked to the town forming a colony which became known as the Newlyn School. Much of their work provides a window on a world hardly changed since the days of the old smugglers.

Not all fishermen were smugglers and when fish stocks were plentiful Newlyn's fishing fleet was kept busy with its lawful occupation. Seafarers were perfectly aware smuggling was unlawful, and detection could result in dire consequences, although it was not considered in any way reprehensible and carried no social stigma in coastal communities like Newlyn.

In January 1794, when John Pollard and his crew of three sailed from Newlyn for Guernsey in his lugger *Lark*, few would have believed his claim of delivering a cargo of *'petates and fish'*. It is unlikely Guernsey had any demand for more potatoes and salt fish than it could produce, but this would hardly have been a bogus voyage. Undoubtedly he did carry those commodities and his given reason probably satisfied the authorities.

There is a new menu every day.
Right: Ben Tunnicliffe, the acclaimed chef-landlord bought the pub in August 2012.

His real purpose of course lay in obtaining a potentially profitable return cargo of contraband brandy, rum or Geneva; together, perhaps, with some tea and tobacco. Written accounts of such expeditions are virtually unknown, and this one is recorded only because the *Lark* was captured by the French frigate *Permone* soon after the outset of their passage.

Life does not get any better than that of a Newlyn cat.

Pollard and his crew were held prisoners of war for nearly two years, during which time the Newlyn captain kept a journal. It opens with the commencement of their fateful trading voyage but unsurprisingly makes no mention of smuggling.

There was nothing novel in Pollard's venture, Mount's Bay fishermen, had smuggling in their

Ben's artist friend
made this pencil
sketch of a winter
storm when waves
smashed through
an upstairs
bedroom window.

These Newlyn
fishermen resting
on a lazy summer
Sunday grew up
listening to their
father's stories of
smuggling days.

blood. Earlier, in February 1751, *'Four Vessels of about ten Tons each'* were reported arriving at Falmouth laden *'with Mackrel, for Guernzey'*. Most probably Mount's Bay luggers or 'mackerel drivers', these relatively small, handy craft of about 15 to 20 tons capacity (or burthen) were well known in Newlyn harbour. They were large enough to carry a modest cargo and sufficiently seaworthy to make the cross-channel passage in comparative safety.

The fishing fleet at Newlyn.

Fishing was the most common pursuit of seafarers, cruising for pleasure was virtually unknown and smuggling was a routine occupation. Throughout this era the trade of larger vessels was heavily regulated. As well as 'charter parties' and cargo 'manifests', there was a system of 'cockets', 'sufferances' and 'coastal dispatches'. Backed by bonds, these provided checks and balances to ensure compliance with marine regulations by merchants, masters and crew alike.

However, much of the smuggling in and around Newlyn involved small fishing boats ferrying contraband from larger sailing ships 'hovering' off shore. Goods were transferred to smaller vessels for offloading on secluded beaches.

Within a certain distance of land 'hovering', defined as loitering with intent at sea, was made illegal in 1736. Newlyn fishermen were not unduly concerned because their everyday occupation provided a perfect alibi. By its very nature, fishing, and especially drift-net fishing, involved putting to sea with no specific destination to spend hours drifting with no discernible intent.

The Tolcarne Inn is a traditional seventeenth-century quayside pub offering exceptionally good food prepared by acclaimed chef-landlord Ben Tunnicliffe who opened in August 2012. Ben's first venture in Cornwall was the Abbey restaurant in Penzance where he was awarded a Michelin Star.

He was later involved in the setting up and opening of the Scarlet Hotel, Mawgan Porth but after two and a half years, keen to set out on his own again, he became aware of the availability of the Tolcarne Inn, just a stone's throw from the fabulous Newlyn fish market, and a most suitable little pub for his vision of affordable and accessible quality food.

Although emphasis is naturally on local seafood, with the menu changing daily, one can still just pop in for a drink. St Austell Tribute, Skinners Betty Stogs and often a local microbrew are on hand pump. A paved courtyard terrace with picnic tables nestles behind the harbour wall which provides essential protection against winter storms, but hides the sea view. Ben regards it philosophically as both a curse and a blessing.

Penzance
Admiral Benbow
46 Chapel Street TR18 4AF

Tel: 01736 363448

Penzance is the principal town of West Penwith, lying in the northwestern corner of Mount's Bay. For centuries it was a remote market town acquiring its living from fishing, mining and smuggling.

In 1748, at Ludgvan, 2 miles northeast of Penzance, Customs Officers could not sell the spirits they seized because of the vast quantity of contraband available at a more competitive price. Smugglers were asking 3/3d a gallon for illegally imported liquor while the reserve price on seized goods was 5/6d.

Penzance Excisemen were ineffective and smugglers had strong local support. In 1770 the Mayor of Penzance was

The seventeenth-century Admiral Benbow in Chapel Street stands on the corner of The Slip leading down to The Quay. The figure lying astride the roof represents Octavius Lanyon, head of the 'Benbow Brandy Men' smuggling gang who operated from the pub during the eighteenth century.

The wonderfully quirky interior houses a fascinating collection of maritime artefacts rescued from numerous shipwrecked vessels.
Below: The Captain's Cabin Restaurant came from a Portuguese Man O' War.

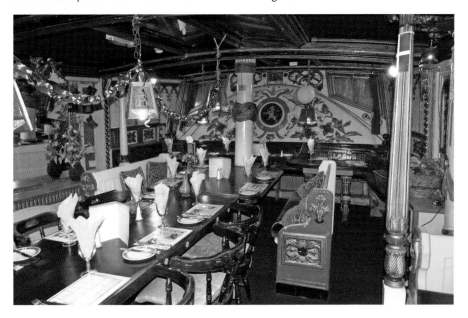

bound over with a large financial surety, to cease smuggling. Three years earlier nine smugglers' vessels, including armed sloops, sailed defiantly from Penzance harbour in broad daylight while a Man O' War looked on, powerless to stop them.

In 1772 a Customs boat from Penzance was plundered and sunk by smugglers, and a smugglers' boat captured Revenue Cutter *Brilliant*, lying in Penzance harbour with seized goods on board. Such stories are numerous in Penzance's history.

The Admiral Benbow has a reputation for good value above average food and well-kept ales such as Sharps, Skinners and St Austell.

The local smuggling gang was known as the 'Benbow Brandy Men' who operated from the Admiral Benbow pub in Chapel Street. The carved wooden figure lying astride the roof of the pub today represents Octavius Lanyon, smuggling chief, who is believed to have climbed onto the roof to create a diversion

Abbey Warehouse where workmen discovered the tunnel leading to The Admiral Benbow.

during a Revenue raid and was shot down and seriously injured.

A few Benbow Brandy Men were captured and their names appear in court records. John Martin, alias Shelly, was indicted together with Walter Cross, James Bell, John Williams, William Bell, William Stone alias Quin and Benjamin Savory:

> ...*being persons of malicious minds and dispositions, &c. after the 1st day of October, 1784, to wit on the 4th of April last, then being on board a certain vessel called the Happy-go-lucky, about two miles from Penzance in Cornwall, with certain guns, to wit, four guns loaded with gun-powder and iron balls, maliciously did shoot at the Hawk Lugger, then being in the service of the King.*

A network of tunnels was discovered a few years ago by builders converting the Abbey Warehouse on the waterfront into a restaurant and offices. A pair of 2 foot square holes with

Upstairs bars have extensive views over Penzance harbour towards St Michael's Mount.

trap doors was found providing access to two tunnels snaking under the roads, one of them leading 300 yards to the Admiral Benbow.

One of the trap doors discovered by workmen leading to a labyrinth of smugglers' tunnels.

Phil Bradby, of developers Mango Homes, was quoted in the local paper as saying:

Smugglers probably built the tunnels with the help of local tin miners. It was amazing. The building was full of debris and rubbish which we were moving out by the skip-load when we found these plates and lifted them up and there were the tunnels.

The world renowned Admiral Benbow is a unique pub and restaurant with a famous history. It houses a fascinating collection of maritime artefacts rescued from numerous ships wrecked on the Cornish coast during the last four hundred years.

Many of the pub's treasures incorporated into the fabric of the building were salvaged over a number of years by deep sea diver Roland Morris who ran an antique shop cum museum on the opposite side of Chapel Street. The Captain's Cabin Restaurant, with its fine woodwork from a Portuguese Man O' War, is an amazing example of Morris' enterprise. The Lady Hamilton lounge features a magnificent cannon and ship's figurehead.

Friendly staff operate this wonderfully quirky seventeenth-century smugglers' pub. The restaurant's full a la carte menu offers a huge variety of good value dishes including local seafood. Vegetarian diners are well catered for with daily specials also available.

The pub's upstairs bars have extensive views over Penzance harbour towards St Michael's Mount. The Admiral Benbow serves a wide variety of fine wines and well-kept real ales such as Sharp's, Skinners and St Austell.

'Them that asks no questions isn't told a lie.'

Rosudgeon
The Falmouth Packet

Packet Lane, Rosudgeon TR20 9QE

Tel: 01736 762240

www.falmouthpacketinn.co.uk

The Falmouth Packet was formerly a coaching inn on the Helston Turnpike.

Rosudgeon is a hamlet in the civil parish of Perranuthnoe just west of the rugged Cudden Point. It is 5 miles east of Penzance and 1 mile north of the isolated rocky shoreline of Prussia Cove. Some years ago an article in *The Cornish Magazine* explained the appeal to smugglers of this inhospitable place:

The pub is named after the Falmouth Packet Service whose ships carried mail to and from the far corners of the British Empire.

...so sheltered and secluded that it is impossible to see what boats are in the little harbour until one literally leans over the edge of the cliff above; a harbour cut out of the solid rock and a roadway with wheel-tracks, partly cut and partly worn, climbing up the face of the cliff on either side of the cove, caves and the remains of caves everywhere, some of them with their mouths built up which are reputed to be connected with the house above by secret passages – these are still existing trademarks left by one of the most enterprising smuggling gangs that Cornwall has ever known.

One of the last Captains of The Falmouth Packet Company, bought the inn in the mid-1850s naming it after the famous shipping service.

Potion No. 9 and Tater-Du are brewed by the nearby Penzance Brewing Company in the village of Crowlas.

Prussia Cove, originally called Porthleah, was renamed in recognition of John Carter, known as the 'King of Prussia', the most successful and notorious smuggler of Penzance district between 1777 and 1807.

According to nineteenth-century historian Sabine Baring-Gould, John Carter earned his nickname as a boy when playing at soldiers with his brothers Harry and Charles, collaborators in the smuggling gang known as 'The Cove Boys'.

For the brothers to succeed in their smuggling business over such a long period, there must have been a degree of intimidation toward the locals. The efficient, profitable smuggling operation was centred on the small inlets of Pisky's Cove and Prussia Cove where they developed the slipways, harbours and roadways

Today the pub consists of a single-room open-plan dining area with L-shaped bar and adjacent conservatory.

Ladies of the Godolphin Cross WI enjoying their Centenary Celebration night at this true community pub.

plus nearby Bessy's Cove where they adapted caves for contraband concealment. Bessy's Cove was named after the lady publican/brewer who kept a 'wink' tavern on the cliff top.

The Carters became so impudent they stationed a battery of guns on top of the cliffs between Bessy's Cove and King's Cove. In one incident they fired a fusillade of shots at a Revenue Cutter. The cutter returned fire but no damage was done to either side.

Despite his reputation as a notorious smuggler, John Carter was known for honest dealing. On one occasion during his absence, the Excise Officers carried off a recently arrived quantity of tea to the Penzance Custom House. On his return, Carter and his men broke into

the stores at night and removed the confiscated cargo, without touching a single article he did not consider his own. He had promised the consignment to a customer and didn't want to break his word.

The conservatory dining room opens on to this sun-trap courtyard.

Some of this enterprising family's fame can be attributed to the autobiography of Harry Carter, one of the few smugglers to leave a first-hand account of his life and activities. *The Autobiography of a Cornish Smuggler*, was first printed in the *Wesley-Methodist Magazine* of October 1831, written after he had seen the light, given up smuggling and retired as a preacher.

His account is sometimes rambling and tedious but sections are lucidly descriptive and give a rare insight into a man

Tracks worn by carts carrying contraband can be clearly seen on the rocks at Prussia Cove.

caught up in a complicated and morally ambiguous profession. On one occasion Harry was tipped off that a bounty of £300 had been put on his head; an astonishingly high sum for the time.

Harry taught himself to read and, perhaps more importantly, to keep his own accounts. Boat owners were known to keep two sets of books, one for the above-board business and one for private perusal only, which must have entailed quite complicated accounting. By his mid-twenties Harry had his own sloop built, followed quickly by a bigger cutter, both providing good service for him, and he recorded: *'By this time I began to think something of myself'.*

This roadway on the cove's western side was created by the Carter smuggling family.

The buildings now comprising The Falmouth Packet Inn stood alongside the main highway from the Falmouth River to Mounts Bay. The Helston Turnpike Trust was created in 1761 to collect tolls used for road maintenance and improvement. The Turnpike or Toll House charges along the highway terminated in 1864.

The Falmouth Packet Shipping Service operated from 1689 until 1850. Ships carried mail to and from the far corners of the British Empire including the West Indies, North and South America, Gibraltar, Malta, Corfu and Britain's longest standing ally, Portugal.

Smugglers' caves at Prussia Cove, some with entrances raised above water level, are reputed to be connected by secret passages to a cliff top house.

The name of this former smugglers' track appears in English and Cornish. Bownder (derived from boundary) means Lane.

One of the last captains of the company retired in 1850 and bought the old hostelry which became established as a coaching inn. In 1873 farmer Thomas Buckett of Carters Down bought the inn and posed for the photograph in his pony and trap.

Today this former inn is a single-room open-plan dining pub with L-shaped bar and an adjacent conservatory. There are some bare stone walls and open fires. It is a real family-run community pub with friendly staff passionate about using local Cornish produce in their meat, fish and vegetarian dishes.

In addition to St Austell's Tribute and Doom Bar are some excellent local ales from The Penzance Brewing Company produced nearby by Pete at The Star Inn in the village of Crowlas. A wonderfully smooth pint, The 'Tater-Du Lighthouse' can be enjoyed on its own or with a tasty organic steak. 'Jolly Farmer' is brewed especially for the pub.

Porthleven
The Ship Inn
Mount Pleasant Road, Porthleven TR13 9JS

Tel: 01326 564204

www.theshipinncornwall.co.uk

This pleasant harbour town, developed in the nineteenth century, has a three-section harbour with wooden bulwarks that can be lowered against storms. The Ship Inn is first mentioned in a 1714 conveyance of Methleigh Manor when it was described as: '...*a new dwelling house with a cellar under, now a public house and held by William Trannick'*. Methleigh Manor dates from 1066 and was held by the Bishop of Exeter. It is half a mile outside the town and reached by way of either the Treza Valley or the cliff road at Breageside.

The two cannon guarding Porthleven Harbour entrance are from the frigate HMS *Anson* wrecked here in 1807.

Around the Cornish coast, the rights to 'Royalty of Wrecks' were often disputed. An example occurred in 1743 at Porthleven when Edward Coode, son of the Lord of Methleigh, hearing of a wreck went to the beach to investigate wearing only a greatcoat and gloves. He was met at the shore by his neighbour Squire Penrose who was accompanied by a gang of armed men. The party defied Coode to touch the cargo and Penrose grabbed a musket crying '*Damn him, shoot him,*

or by God, I'll shoot him'. Ironically, all they were fighting over was a case of salted pork.

In 1768 Excise Officer William Odgers was brutally murdered by smugglers at Porthleven. A Gwennap man, Melchisideck Kinsman, was accused of the murder, together with other persons unknown. His accomplices were initially thought to have fled to Guernsey or Morlaix, but were later reported to be hiding in the tin mines.

The gang offered a bribe of £500 to the principal witness to go abroad. When this inducement failed he was threatened with violence. In fear for his life the hapless informer was unable to work and was later awarded a state pension of seven shillings a week.

Three of Kinsman's accomplices eventually surrendered and, presumably in exchange for a pardon or leniency, agreed to track him down. Kinsman was caught and all four stood trial at the assizes. However, it was only the judge who was astonished when none was found guilty. The local Collector of Customs observed that three of the jury had disappeared after the trial, and suggested they had been either bribed or 'nobbled'. Two years later another Customs Officer commented:

...nobody can venture to come near (the smugglers) with safety while they are at their work.

He told the missus he was *'just popping out for a swift half!'*

In 1790 the village consisted of about sixty cottages. Alice Stodden was running The Ship when the sale of *'shares in a*

The Ship's main bar is packed full of interest from floor to ceiling.

Oliver the land-lord, pulling a pint of Porthleven, says a section of the cellar wall looks as though it could conceal a tunnel entrance or store.

seine' was held there. The term seine refers to a combination of boats, nets and fishing gear. In 1810 Joseph Glasson leased the pub from Edward Coode and following Glasson's death his widow Mary took charge and remained landlady for over thirty-five years.

The Old Customs' House on the opposite side of the harbour func-tions today as a gallery.

Among subsequent landlords recorded in the licensing lists was Joseph Gilbert, who in 1877 was charged with *'Keeping his house open for the sale of beer on Good Friday night and before four o'clock on the Saturday morning'*. By 1879 the landlord was William Mildren whose five-year-old son was tragically drowned in the harbour.

In 1884 the Austrian barque *Civiet* was driven onto Porthleven beach. The captain and two of the crew were swept into the sea but the remainder owed their lives to Joseph Gilbert who succeeded in hurling a lifeline to the ship enabling the men to struggle ashore.

There are persistent, unconfirmed rumours that the pub's cellar was linked by a tunnel to Methleigh Manor. However, the only tunnels to have been discovered are those that channel water from the hills down to the mill. When dry these conduits could have been used for storing contraband.

Porthleven on a peaceful day. The three section harbour has wooden bulwarks that are lowered when storms threaten.

In a storm like this, Joseph Gilbert landlord of The Ship succeeded in hurling a life-line to men aboard the stricken Austrian barque *Civiet*.

Oliver, the present landlord of The Ship, says an area of cellar wall appears to have been bricked up and an elderly local man has recalled how, while standing in the cellar a draft of air drew the smoke from his pipe into a fissure in the rock wall.

There are also rumoured to be further smugglers' tunnels connected to caves in the harbour area and elsewhere on the coast nearby. The cliffs where some of them terminated are the site of many graves of drowned sailors. Since there was no way of determining whether these victims were Christian they were not entitled to burial in a churchyard.

The Ship Inn is a real Cornish pub built into rocks at the entrance of Porthleven harbour. The adjacent former Smithy provides an ideal family/children's room, as well as an outdoor area for rain free days!

During winter, two log fires warm the pub interior, while flames from a third, flicker in the family room. Windows in the pub's candle-lit dining room overlook the harbour. Honest bar food includes good crab sandwiches and home-made pies plus prawn mornay and smoked fish platter. The varying range of real ales often includes Rebel Gold from the micro-brewery of that name in Penryn.

The coast path above Porthleven Beach where Customs Riding Officers patrolled nightly in all weathers on the lookout for smugglers.

Helston
Blue Anchor

50 Coinagehall Street, Helston TR13 8EL

Tel: 01326 562821

www.spingoales.com

The Blue Anchor dating from the fifteenth century is one of the oldest original inns in Britain.

Located at the northern end of the Lizard peninsula, Helston is 13 miles from the port towns of Penzance in the west and Falmouth in the east. Although difficult to imagine today, Helston was a very busy port in its own right until the thirteenth century when a shingle bar formed across the mouth of the River Cober, preventing access to the sea. Afterwards

The small rooms off the central passage would have been perfect for Christopher Wallis's conferences with smugglers and customers.

goods were transported to a new quay at Gweek, until further silting and a decline in tin extraction ended the trade.

Helston is the westernmost of Cornwall's five medieval Stannary towns where 'streamed tin' extracted from river valleys was taken for quality assaying and taxing before being despatched throughout southern Britain and continental Europe. Over the centuries the meaning of the terms Excise and Customs have become blurred. Customs is the tax levied on imported goods while Excise charges are imposed on exports.

Export duty applied initially to wool and resulted in the first smugglers of Kent and Sussex. When later imposed on metals, particularly tin, it had a great impact on

The stone staircase at the end of the corridor leads to the brewery.

Spingo is produced in a variety of strengths. The most popular is Middle at 5.0% and for the brave there is Special at 6.5%. At Christmas and Easter, an extra special brew is available at 7.6% ABV.

The front bar of this no-nonsense pub with its well-worn furniture.

Below: Friendly locals relaxing in the cosy back bar.

Cornwall. Helston's first smugglers were engaged in export-
ing untaxed tin.

Christopher Wallis, a very successful Helston attorney, regularly managed the affairs of local smugglers and privateers.
He acted for the salvors in many wreck cases, and as the local
agent for a number of the Guernsey merchant houses.
Although a qualified lawyer, Wallis was once prosecuted for
a smuggling related offence.

Like many of his standing he enjoyed the finer elements of
life and entertained others of the Helston gentry. From his
journal we learn he was at Bochym on 10 October 1781 when
he: 'dined with Messrs. Glynn, Grenfell, Wills, Mr. Sandys, Mr.
Collector Johns, Isaac Head, Messrs Pasmore, Farnham, Cove, &
Hellings, Mr. S. Sandys, Mr. H. Sandys, Mr. Wills Jun'r, Mr.
Michell, Mr. Wm. Tremayne, Mr. Scobell, my brother John & others
- drank freely.'

Messrs Johns, Head, Pasmore and Scobell were Collectors of
Customs for Falmouth, Gweek, Scilly, and Penzance respec-
tively, while others were magistrates, merchants, agents and
bankers not completely removed from smuggling.

It was well understood that Cornish juries hardly ever
convicted Cornish smugglers. That was why, in 1799 a case
involving Helston smugglers was heard at the Old Bailey.
Court records of the time provide a fascinating first-hand
account of an incident that took place on 21 December outside
the town. Acting on a tip off, Preventive Officer William
Mitchell of Helston, laid an ambush for a gang of local smugglers. Around nine o'clock on a bright moonlight night
Mitchell's men waited behind a field gate at the side of a

known contraband trail. The free traders were all mounted, the first to gallop past being John Skinner, though he carried nothing with him.

Mitchell knew most of the smugglers by name and shouted a challenge, calling them to give up peaceably which they ignored. The next to gallop up were Barnard and Pascoe, each

Helston was a very busy port until the thirteenth century when a shingle bar formed across the mouth of the River Cober, preventing access to the sea.

with two 7-gallon casks of liquor attached by cords and slung over their horses. When Mitchell attempted to stop them he was violently assaulted:

> ...they instantly struck at me a number of blows with large sticks; I had one blow over my eye, that I thought I had lost the sight of my eye; I was under the doctor's hands a long time; and

*another across the nose; there were a great many other blows…
I lost a great deal of blood; the wound on my eye was a very
deep one. Pascoe's stick appeared to be four feet and a half long,
and a large head to it; after he had got over the gate, he took both
hands and struck me repeatedly.*

Now you know
why it is called a
settle!

Most of the smugglers
escaped but Barnard was
hit on the head by officer
Samuel Parnell who caught
him by the collar, secured
him, and took him off to
Helston. Mitchell, who had
three loaded pistols about
him said: '*I was loth to make
use of them; if I had, I think, as
we were so close, it must have
taken the life of one of them*'.
He did not draw the pistols
until approaching Helston on the return when he became
fearful of a rescue attempt.

When Mitchell later remonstrated with Barnard for using him
so ill the smuggler said: '*he was very sorry for it, and begged we
would let him go; and he said, if he had known they were Helston
officers, he would not have hurt them; but he thought they were
Penryn officers, otherwise they should not have acted in the manner
they did*'.

Parnell was also injured in the fracas receiving a cut across
the back of his hand severing the tendons to his fingers. A
'curious' knife, possibly a cutlass, was found the next
morning by the farmer who handed it to the smugglers.

Barnard was found guilty and sentenced to two years hard labour on board one of the filthy prison hulks moored in the Thames estuary.

There can be little doubt that Barnard, Pascoe, Skinner and others were patrons of the Blue Anchor, one of the oldest original inns in Britain. The ancient thatched hostelry is located towards the bottom of Coinagehall Street; the main high street of the town.

Dating from the fifteenth century, the pub still maintains a working brewery. A hundred years ago the inn became so popular with local tin miners they were paid their wages at the bar. Originally a monks' rest house for pilgrims, the inn produced a strong honey-based mead. Today it produces 'Spingo Ale' in the brewery located at the rear of the premises alongside the old skittle alley.

The Blue Anchor is one of the oldest original inns in Britain.

97

For about five-
hundred years
Halzephron Inn
has stood here on
Gunwalloe shore
defiantly facing
the ferocity of
westerly storms
and gales.

Gunwalloe
Halzephron Inn
Gunwalloe, Helston TR12 7QB

Tel: 01326 240406

www.halzephron-inn.co.uk

The small community of Gunwalloe with its scattering of fishermen's cottages is situated on the eastern tip of Mount's Bay
where the storm battered coast sweeps down towards Lizard
Point. Originally owned by the Penrose family, Gunwalloe
village was eventually sold, mostly to sitting tenants and the
National Trust.

The tales of ships lost in this location and of the wrecking
activities of the local 'country people' are so numerous they
could fill a separate book. One vicar whose Sunday service
was interrupted by a man announcing a wreck on nearby
rocks is said to have begged the congregation to remain

seated until he'd taken off his cassock *'so that we can all start fair'*. In 1739 Reverend Thomas Whitford, rector of nearby Cury, was caught by Customs Men in possession of four casks of wine looted from the wreck of *The Lady Lucy*.

Some of the most notable shipwrecks at Gunwalloe include *The St Anthony*, a treasure ship belonging to the King of Portugal which was wrecked in the cove in 1527. After tramping half a mile across the cliffs to join in the wrecking, patrons of the Halzephron Inn later passed plundered Portuguese dollars across the bar in exchange for brandy.

The name Halzephron comes from Old Cornish for 'Hell's Cliff'.

The false wall between the Lounge and the Fishermans Bar is 8'6" thick concealing a secret shaft.

In 1676 a Spanish galleon worth two million pounds was wrecked here and in 1684 *The Schiedam*, a Dutch ship of 400 tons, apparently transporting cannon for the English army from Tangier to Portsmouth, was also lost. In 1785, a ship carrying a consignment of silver dollars ran aground at Church Cove, a place still popular with treasure hunters who can be seen combing the sandy beach with metal detectors. In 1790 yet another bullion ship, carrying seventeen million dollars from Spanish Bankers foundered in nearby 'Dollar' Cove.

This trapdoor in the loft gives access to the smugglers' escape route.

The charming little church of St Winwalloe, which gives Church Cove its name, lies protected in the sand dunes behind a cliff. Known as 'The Church of the Storms', it has a separate stand-alone bell tower and is

Below: Sharp's Doom Bar plus Skinners Betty Stogs and Porthleven are on hand pump.

Several dining areas include cosy nooks.

surrounded by a tamarisk hedge. The church was rebuilt in the fifteenth century on the site of an earlier place of worship and is named after a little-known sixth-century Breton Abbot.

Gunwalloe possessed several good beaches and coves for landing contraband. Caves on the main beach were said to be linked by a tunnel to St Winwalloe's belfry, while another

Seating up to thirty people, the main dining room displays pictures of sailing ships and lots of gleaming copper on its whitewashed stone walls.

101

passage joined the Halzephron Inn to 'Fishing Cove', the home of a fascinating local smuggler Henry Cuttance, listed in the 1851 census as a victualler born at St Keverne. By the 1840s he was landlord of an inn at Gunwalloe and running a small but profitable smuggling operation on the side. He acted as a smuggler, seller and distributor of contraband.

Cuttance was once seized by a press gang and taken away to a man-of-war but escaped by throwing his hat off one side of the ship and shouting 'man overboard!' As everyone rushed to help, he quietly slipped over the other side and swam the 3 miles back to shore.

The smuggling landlord was among the brave men risking their own lives to rescue the master and three crew of the

St Winwalloes's 'The Church of the Storms' sheltering in the lee of Church Cove Hill.

Norwegian schooner *Elizabeth*, of Bergen, wrecked at Gunwalloe. The account of the rescue came to the attention of the King of Norway who initiated a silver cup to be presented to the innkeeper with the etched transcription: *'Oscar, King of Norway, to Henry Cuttance of Gunwalloe, For brave and noble actions on the 20 Nov., 1846'.*

For about five hundred years the Halzephron Inn has stood here on the Gunwalloe shore defiantly facing the ferocity of westerly storms and gales. The name Halzephron comes from Old Cornish for 'Hell's Cliff'. The inn sign depicts a sailing ship being dashed on the rocks and indeed a number of local wrecks provided many of the timbers in this inn.

The wall between the Lounge and the Fishermans Bar is 8'6" thick and conceals a shaft leading to a tunnel which at one time connected the inn to a nearby monastery.

The smugglers' landing beach at Church Cove.

The pub closed during the First World War and remained shut throughout the Second World War, reopening only in the late fifties when families were beginning to afford cars and seaside holidays.

In the 1790s artist George Morland produced a series of paintings of smugglers landing contraband.

The neatly-kept bar rooms have an informal friendly atmosphere and are decorated with lots of local pictures. There are a number of dining areas including cosy nooks. The main dining room, seating up to thirty people, has pictures of sailing ships on its whitewashed stone walls and lots of gleaming copper. Sharp's Doom Bar plus Skinners Betty Stogs and Porthleven are on hand pump. Also available are nine wines by the glass and 40 malt whiskies.

Picnic tables at the front of the inn provide panoramic views across National Trust fields and the whole expanse of Mounts Bay. The South West Coast Path heading north traverses the mile long beach from Fishing Cove to Porthleven and heading south, leads to Church Cove and beyond.

Mullion
Old Inn
Churchtown, Mullion TR12 7HN

Tel: 01326 240240

www.oldinnmullion.co.uk

The sixteenth-century Old Inn is a traditional thatched and beamed pub located in the heart of Mullion village.

Mullion Cove, formerly Porth Mellin, is another small inlet on the Lizard peninsula. Facing west into Mount's Bay it is approximately 6 miles south of Helston and a mile southwest of Mullion village. Unlike other coves on this stretch of coast Mullion has a small harbour. Completed in 1895 and financed by Lord Robartes of Lanhydrock it was a gesture to recompense the Mullion fishermen who had suffered several disastrous pilchard seasons.

The pub comprises a number of characterful linked dining areas.

The harbour is protected from southerly gales by two sea walls and by Mullion Island, half a mile offshore. In 1945 the harbour, with its old pilchard cellar and net store, and the

island were donated to the National Trust by the Meyer family.

Mullion Cove was a favourite landing place for contraband with virtually the whole population involved as local historian Reverend E. G. Harvey confirmed when writing in 1875:

> *During the last century, and the early part of this, it is said there was hardly a family in these parts that was not more or less concerned in the trade; and men living may even now, so far from considering it a disgrace, be heard to speak proudly of the day when they were engaged in the smuggling service.*

This former inglenook provides a snug corner.
Above right: Children are welcome in the family dining area.

On a June night in 1801 a boat's crew from HM Gun Vessel *Hecate*, boarded and seized a contraband-laden smuggling lugger which had run ashore at Mullion. When news of this disaster spread the locals raided an armoury at Trenance and made off with a supply of muskets and ammunition. Taking position on a cliff above the lugger they opened fire and the naval party were forced to quit the prize and take to their boat.

One of the main protagonists in the fracas was William Richards, alias Billy Payow, believed to be part owner of the lugger or her cargo. The King's Pardon was offered to any smuggler (except Richards) for giving information on the Mullion musket-men. The Lords Commissioners of the Admiralty added a reward of £100. Some of the most respectable persons in the parish were also engaged in this affair and although they were threatened with prosecution, the Rev. Harvey indicates the matter was hushed up.

The prestigious Cask Marque has been awarded to the St Austell ales.

Another story involved a prominent local smuggler known as 'the Spotsman' (the crewman in charge of the cargo who selected the exact spot on the coast where it was to be landed). Despite several encounters with Revenue Cutters and Coastguards, he had completed many successful round trips to France. On one occasion returning home he landed a cargo of brandy at a spot known as 'The Chair', between Predannack Head and Mullion Cove. However, his waiting friends were about to fire a furze beacon to warn him Customs Men had organized a reception committee. A mad scramble back to the cliffs saved the day and the tubs were quietly moved off the rocks to a nearby mineshaft.

Mullion's small harbour was completed in 1895 as an aid to poor fishing families.

When the Customs Men arrived the beach was deserted, and despite coming within a hundred yards of the hidden contraband, the Preventive Men were deceived, and only had the seized smugglers' boat to show for the night's work. After the officers departed the smugglers recovered their property undetected. Two tubs that had floated free were later picked up by a friendly fishing boat.

The Spotsman was fortunate to escape capture or injury on that particular run but he wasn't always so lucky. On another occasion he was mistaken for a Revenue Man when he was slow to reply to a challenge from another smuggler. He was shot at but fortunately lost only his thumb in the encounter.

Thomas Rowlandson's 1810 sketch of smugglers in a cove on the Cornish coast is a contemporary depiction of the free traders at work.

By 1824 the tide was turning against the smugglers and a Coastguard Station was built at Mullion Cove. Lieutenant Drew, the chief Coastguard for the Mullion area is credited with smashing the local smuggling ring. On one occasion Drew and a fellow Coastguard Officer interrupted a run but the smugglers melted away into the night. The two Preventive Men clambered to the beach to find a rope leading out to sea and, pulling together, they hauled in 100 sunken tubs.

On 4 May 1859, the first train of Isambard Kingdom Brunel's railway, made the journey from Plymouth across the Tamar River and into the former secretive county. A tourist industry began to develop and guide books and travel diaries were published. This initiative established a wide reputation for the generous hospitality of Miss Mary Munday of the Old Inn at Mullion.

Most Victorian tourists were unaware the Mundays were one of the foremost smuggling families of the area. John Munday, together with accomplice Bobo George, stored their contraband in a cavern at the cove, accessible only at low tide. It is rumoured a tunnel led from the cave to a cliff-top farm.

The sixteenth-century Old Inn is a traditional thatched and beamed pub located in the heart of Mullion village. There is a central carvery serving generous good food from doorstep sandwiches to pies and evening steaks.

The Old Inn is a St Austell Brewery pub stocking Tribute as well as two other St Austell beers, plus a guest beer. They hold the prestigious Cask Marque, reflecting the care they take of their beer and cellar management: there are plenty of decent wines available by the glass.

The inside dining areas display lots of brasses, plates, clocks, nautical items and old wreck pictures. In summer there are picnic sets on the terrace and garden and for the winter there is a large inglenook fireplace. Accommodation is provided in the roomy Victorian extension.

John Munday and Bobo George used a cavern at the cove as a contraband store.

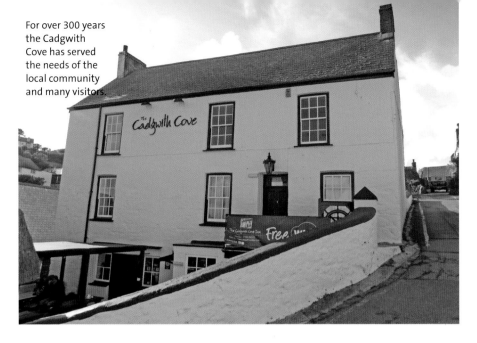

For over 300 years the Cadgwith Cove has served the needs of the local community and many visitors.

Cadgwith
The Cadgwith Cove

Cadgwith, Ruan Minor TR12 7JX

Tel: 01326 290513

www.cadgwithcoveinn.com

Otter Bitter, Sharp's Doom Bar, Skinners Betty Stogs and a varying guest ale are on hand pump.

Just around the tip of the Lizard peninsula lies the tiny unspoilt working fishing village of Cadgwith. Positioned on the South West Coastal Path, Cadgwith is set against a backdrop of pastel coloured and whitewashed cottages, many of them thatched, spilling down to the cove. This once thriving centre of the pilchard trade holds the record for the most caught in a day: 1.3 million. Today the fishermen depend on catches of crabs and lobsters.

Smuggling was so prevalent here that Customs authorities set up an establishment to combat it as early as 1778. At the time it was said: *'It is common for the inhabitants to take in and secrete smuggled goods for capital smugglers who frequently land cargoes'.*

Several accounts of smuggling were reported in the *Royal Cornwall Gazette*, including an incident on 4 February 1815 when Customs Officers stationed here seized 45 ankers of brandy on the beach, where presumably they had been abandoned by free traders disturbed in the act of landing them. In another incident two years later, in March, the officer of the Cadgwith Preventive boat seized an even bigger haul of 150 ankers of brandy which had been sunk nearby.

Painted picnic sets on the good-sized front terrace overlook fish sheds and the cove.

The pretty little fishing cove of Coverack, 3 miles north-east also witnessed some lively smuggling events. The Cadgwith and Coverack Preventive boats, working together with grappling irons on 14 March 1822, 'crept up' 94 kegs of contraband spirits, near the Lizard, which were taken to the Custom House in Falmouth. A Custom House boat belonging to the

Visitors and residents mix happily in this village community pub.

The dining room walls are decorated with lots of local photographs.

On 4 February 1815 Customs Officers seized 45 ankers of brandy landed on the beach within sight of the pub.

port of Gweek was stationed at Coverack and commanded by Captain Thomas. On 27 December 1815 Thomas succeeded in capturing a Coverack smuggling vessel found to have 150 ankers of spirits on board. The crew escaped in their small boat.

Christopher Wallis, a very successful Helston attorney, regularly bought wine and spirits from the Coverack and Cadgwith smugglers. One of his journal entries confirms he purchased: '… *at Cadgwith 2 Quarter Casks Port at 5 G.s just then come onshore – p'd J. Randle 5 G'n*'. And again in September 1795: '*Rec'd p'Thos Richards from Edw'd Richards Ruan Minor, an anker of Brandy and an anker of Geneva - the price at Cadgwith Cove said now to be £3 11s 0d*'.

Over 300 years old, The Cadgwith Cove has remained largely unspoilt since the old smuggling days. The bars are full of atmosphere and relics collected throughout a rich seafaring history, adorn the walls of the bar. The two snugly-dark front rooms house plain pub furnishings on parquet floors, which are often happily tested with dogs and muddy boots.

Today fishermen of Cadgwith catch crabs and lobster which feature prominently on the pub's menu.

There is a log fire in the dining room. Cases of naval hat ribbons and cabinets displaying fancy knot-work share the wall space with photographs including some of local gig races. A couple of compass binnacles are included and some of the dark beams are decked out with ships' shields. A back bar has a huge, colourful fish mural.

Otter Bitter, Sharp's Doom Bar, Skinners Betty Stogs and a varying guest ale are on hand pump. Lunch and dinner are served with a range of home-produced food and fresh seafood including lobster sourced from the cove.

Painted picnic sets, some under a fairy-lit awning, adorn an extensive front terrace with views across fish sheds to the cove. Excellent cliff walks lead off in either direction from this bustling heart of the village community.

In 1781, William Wallis, the corrupt attorney from Helston, purchased port, gin and brandy from the Cadgwith smugglers.
(Courtesy of Buckler's Hard Maritime Museum)

Porthallow
The Five Pilchards Inn
Porthallow, Helston TR12 6PP

Tel: 01326 280256

www.thefivepilchards.co.uk

The Five Pilchards free house has stood in its location at top of Porthallow beach for around three hundred years.

Porthallow (known locally as 'Pralla') is another of the small, former pilchard fishing communities facing Falmouth Bay. Today fishing continues on a much smaller scale with smuggling an ingrained part of the folklore. The beach, once frequented by free traders, now attracts geologists from far and wide as it lies on the glacial fault line.

In the 1970s, *The Porthallow Village Association* was established to buy the beach from the Trelowarren Estate.

Landlord David Lambrick, a former St Keverne farmer and award-winning cheesemaker, began running The Five Pilchards in April 2009.

The group of local investors also raised sufficient money to purchase the building formerly used to cure pilchards and to convert it into a village hall.

Throughout the eighteenth and first half of the nineteenth century the whole of the Lizard peninsula was a hotbed of smuggling. Isolated beachside locations like Porthallow, Coverack and Cadgwith, which are accessible only down narrow lanes, were little worlds within a world. By the very nature of these places; quiet creeks, porths and backwater havens, the secretive business of smuggling could take hold and flourish.

Although now open-plan, the pub's original separate room locations are easily discernible and form distinct drinking and eating areas.

In addition to the remote location, another factor working in favour of Porthallow and Coverack smugglers was the great volume of passing shipping, particularly vessels bound for

The old stone fireplace has been adapted to house a wood-burning stove for winter months. The enormous scale model on the mantelshelf is of a local harbour tug.

Falmouth. This made identification of a suspicious sail a matter of some difficulty both for patrolling Revenue cruisers and officers of the land-based Preventive Service.

Falmouth, as the main port of the area, was the Custom House centre whose official limits extended some way along the coast on either side. Porthallow was sufficiently distant to avoid much scrutiny and smugglers were able to transport contraband north round St Anthony's Head and up the tidal Helford River to the ready markets of Gweek and Helston. The beautiful tree-lined Helford estuary offered a perfect haven for smugglers, its winding creeks and concealed hiding places providing excellent cover for illicit operations.

One contemporary report is rather amusing: '*An officer of the Customs of the Port of Gweek was lately a cock shooting, he marked a bird into a covert, where, on approaching to flush it, he discovered a 'covey', consisting of 63 ankers of brandy; the whole of which he secured without firing a shot*'.

In the 1970s members of the community clubbed together to buy Porthallow beach from the Trelowarren Estate allowing it to remain completely unspoilt.

The Manacles (deriving from the Cornish Meyn Eglos meaning church stones) are a set of treacherous rocks in Falmouth Bay about 1 nautical mile southeast of Porthallow. The reef consists of many submerged rocks and several groups that break the surface – although some only at low water. There have been over a thousand lives lost from more than one hundred ship-wrecks here. Today it is a popular spot for diving with many of the well-known wrecks in a central concentrated group 300 x 200 metres, and less than 6 metres deep.

When sailing south to the Channel Islands or Roscoff to buy contraband, the smugglers of Porthallow had to negotiate a safe route around the dreaded Mana-cles. The two man crew of a smuggling boat was captured off the Manacles in June 1836 by the Cover-ack Preventive boat *Active*. The fifty kegs of spirits they had on board were lodged in the King's Ware-house at Falmouth. On 22 April 1822 two smuggling vessels returning from France were lost near the Manacles. Both boats were supposed to have foundered and their crews drowned. A French fishing vessel picked up several kegs of spirits in the area together with parts of the boats.

In January 1882 the pub was 'newly built' as an extension to an existing forge and stable. The wonky fanlight over the back door to the yard suggests a much earlier date.

The Five Pilchards free house is located at the top of Porthal-low beach. The name 'Five Pilchards' (Pymp Hernen in Cornish) is derived from the traditional custom of counting pilchards in groups of five.

The pub is believed to be over 300 years old but documenta-tion confirming its exact age is hard to come by. The present building is an extension of an older one, incorporating the original forge and stable. The documented history of the Five

Pilchards can be traced to at least the 1830s. On the wall of the bar is a framed list of landlords going back nearly 250 years. The nineteenth-century innkeepers were John Bryant (who was here for thirty-nine years from 1833), John Martin, Thomas Pearce and Samuel Southey.

Although now open-plan, the pub's original separate room locations are easily discernible and form distinct drinking and eating areas, furnished with wooden settles, tables and chairs. The bar area with wood-planked floor and beamed ceiling is bedecked with nautical bric-à-brac of all kinds and dominated by enormous scale models of a lifeboat and local harbour tugs.

I had thought a 'Fisherman's Friend' was a throat lozenge until I discovered Porthallow.

The old stone fireplace has been adapted to house a wood-burning stove for the winter months. Food is a significant part of the service here, ranging from sandwiches and snacks to main meals. There are up to three ales offered in summer, always one from the Sharp's Brewery range and two or three ever-changing guest beers.

The freshest of fish dishes include Porthallow lobster thermidor, Cadgwith crab bake, chargrilled cod burger, crispy panko squid with sweet chilli mayo, king prawn red Thai curry and herb crusted hake.

Perched on the water's edge The Shipwrights Arms has uninterrupted views across the beautiful Helford estuary.

Helford Village
The Shipwrights Arms
Helford, Helston TR12 6JX

Tel: 01326 231235

www.shipwrightshelford.co.uk

The Helford River is a large estuary located snugly between the western edge of Falmouth Bay and eastern side of the Lizard peninsula. This popular tourist destination is renowned for its scenic beauty and marine ecology. Today it is a haven for yachtsmen but two-hundred years ago the creeks proved very useful to smugglers seeking privacy for their clandestine activities.

The timewarp village of Helford is a photographers' delight where cottages perched on the waterfront have dinghies moored outside and boat houses instead of car ports. A passenger ferry provides an alternative to approaching along the maze of twisting lanes through Gweek, Mawgan and Manaccan. Capable of transporting 12 people it leaves 'on request' from the Ferryboat Inn on the northern shore. A large hinged coloured disc, mounted on a pole on the southern shore, is opened up as a signal to the ferryman that passengers are ready for the return trip.

Harry Carter of Prussia Cove was a member of one of the most notorious smuggling families active in the late eighteenth century. Much of what is known about his exploits and those of his infamous brothers comes from his life story published as: *The Autobiography of a Cornish Smuggler*. From this we learn he married a Helford girl:

Two regular real ales are supplemented by a guest beer, often from Lizard Brewery.

> '*In the year of 19th April, 1786, I was married to Elizabeth Flindel, of Helford, in the parish of Manaccan, and in April 19, in 1787, she bore me a daughter, who was called after her mother's name, and I think it was about middle of November*'.

The Helford free traders were remarkably daring, and pursued their activities even in the face of stiff opposition.

The pleasantly decorated single lounge bar has an informal nautical theme.

121

Early in September 1840, a vessel called the *Teignmouth* was seized at Gweek by Coastguard Officers of the Coverack Station. Lashed to the outside of the vessel were 133 half ankers of brandy; a technique more usually associated with Kent smugglers where the sea crossing was much shorter.

The restaurant's window overlooks the wide expanse of the estuary.

On approaching Gweek, the crew of the *Teignmouth* hailed two men on the beach for help in drawing the kegs ashore. Unfortunately they turned out to be armed Customs Officers who drew their pistols and arrested the smugglers. The contraband was seized and transported to the Customs House at Helford.

A few days later, in the early hours of the morning, a 30-strong gang of smugglers with appropriated horses and carts broke open the Customs House and retrieved their goods. The gang worked quickly from 1 to 1.30 am and generously left three barrels behind for the Excisemen. The officer on station heard the doors being forced, but was powerless to intervene as the nearest dwelling was half a mile away in the village.

In April 2012 a local consortium bought and re-opened this classic waterside venue.

This small thatched village pub, dating from the eighteenth century, occupies a delightful spot on Helford River's south bank. The terraced patio gardens which drop down to palm trees at the water's edge provide a view of the beautiful wooded creek. Conveniently located picnic tables greatly increase the pub's capacity.

The Shipwrights Arms was put up for sale in November 2008

but failed to find a buyer and fell into liquidation the following year. In April 2012 a local consortium bought and re-opened this classic waterside venue. Very limited parking is a further reason to consider approaching by passenger ferry.

A passenger ferry leaves 'on request' from the Ferry-boat Inn on the northern shore.

The pleasantly-decorated single lounge bar with a nautical theme offers two regular real ales supplemented by a guest beer, often from Lizard Brewery. The restaurant's picture window overlooks the wide expanse of the estuary. Changing every day, the small, imaginative menu naturally features fish fresh from the Helford River. Lunches including salads and steaks are always available with at least one vegetarian option. In high summer the pub runs a charcoal BBQ in the terrace garden.

The former Customs building stands in isolation by the ruins of an old fort along the coastal path half a mile from the village.

123

This busy old-fashioned place occupies a prime spot on Custom House Quay with views across the harbour.

Falmouth
The Chain Locker

Custom House Quay, Quay Street, Falmouth TR11 3HH

Tel: 01326 311085

Located at the entrance to Carrick Roads, Falmouth has a spectacular deep water anchorage formed by the merging of seven river estuaries. In 1660, when The Chain Locker was established, Falmouth was a small village of little consequence. Things changed dramatically in 1661 following receipt of the town charter and in 1668, the Post Office decided to site the 'Packet Station' for international mail services here.

For over 160 years, throughout the smuggling era, Falmouth became the centre of international communications between Britain's allies and Atlantic colonies. At its peak over forty

Packet vessels worked out of Falmouth ferrying mail, official dispatches, passengers and bullion to countries including America, Jamaica, Barbados, Mexico, Brazil, Spain, Portugal, Malta and Madeira.

New inns were built in the town and established places like The Chain Locker were extended for the accommodation of travellers. At the height of the Packet Service in 1802 Robert Southey wrote of his experience:

The perpetual stir and bustle in this inn is as surprising as it is wearisome. Doors opening shutting, bells ringing, voices calling to the waiter from every quarter, while he cries, 'coming' to one room and hurries away to another. Everybody is in a hurry here, either they are going off to the packets and are hastening their preparations to embark, or they have just arrived and are impatient to be on the road homeward. Every now and then a carriage rattles up to the door with a rapidity which makes the very house shake...

This painting is of the eighteenth-century harbour. When The Chain Locker was established in 1660, Falmouth was a small village of little consequence.

Falmouth is located in a magnificent position at the entrance to Carrick Roads, a spectacular deep water anchorage formed by the merging of seven river estuaries.

As the number of Packet vessels increased local tradesmen prospered creating constant demands on a whole range of goods; many readily supplied by smugglers. From the beginning, captains and crews freely indulged in smuggling and as they were poorly paid the practice was considered as perks and the goods were exempt from Customs checks. Inevitably this privilege was grossly abused and large quantities of contraband were openly brought ashore. Eventually the Board of Customs made representations to the Post Office concerning this loss of revenue and several Packets were seized. The Packet Service was reorganised in 1789 causing the crews to mutiny as they could not subsist solely on their regular pay of 23 shillings a month. To suppress the revolt the Post Office was obliged to raise the amount to 28 shillings plus a daily food allowance of ninepence.

As I write The Chain Locker boasts one of the best selection of real ales in Cornwall.

It was not only Packet boats that were involved in smuggling. In 1762 three East Indiamen returning to Britain from China anchoring in the bay for a fortnight held a regular on board

Many a yarn has been told here. Many ships' crews have sung their songs here. History hangs on walls, friezes and ceilings in the bars.

bazaar, selling silk, muslin, dimities (squares of light strong cotton fabric), china, tea, arrack, handkerchiefs and other goods.

Newspaper reports of 24 May 1839 tell of a schooner loaded with coal moored in the harbour. As the cargo was gradually unloaded a suspicious Customs Officer bored a small hole in the side of the ship. On withdrawing the gimlet he received a face-full of brandy from a tub stowed in a cavity between the false interior of the hull and the outside. Altogether 276 concealed barrels of brandy and gin were discovered. The ship had been operating for three years without detection.

Much of the contraband brought ashore from East Indiamen, Post Office Packets and other shipping went directly into warehouses of reputable merchants from where it would be purchased by members of the Cornish gentry. Revenue Officers were prepared to turn a blind eye in return for a share of the proceeds.

This busy old-fashioned place stands in a prime spot on Custom House Quay with views across the harbour. Many a yarn has been told here. Many ships' crews have sung their

Above left:
Numerous nooks and crannies are decorated with nautical bric-a-brac and local pictures.

Above right:
Inside the floors are slate or bare boards and the walls are a gallery of local maritime images.

The Old Customs House on the corner of Arwenack Street and Quay Street is now a restaurant called The Stables.

songs here. History hangs on walls, friezes and ceilings in the bars. There are a number of window tables and lots of outside seating providing a great location to watch the world go by.

The pub presently boasts one of the largest selections of real ales in Cornwall. They serve generous food from sandwiches and baguettes to local fish dishes. Inside the floors are slate or bare boards with numerous nooks and crannies decorated with nautical bric-a-brac and local maritime pictures.

As I write, St Austell Brewery has just acquired this historic pub so some things are bound to change. However, Adam Luck estate director for St Austell Brewery sounds positive:

While retaining the charm and heritage of The Chain Locker, we aim to breathe new life into the adjoining redundant buildings which were formerly the Shipwrights and Marine Restaurant to make the most of their prime waterside position.